Z is for Zeus

A Greek Mythology Alphabet

Written by Helen L. Wilbur and Illustrated by Victor Juhasz

To the Wilbur men—Wayne, Glenn, Dave, Steve, Tom, and remembering Nac.

HELEN

For my sons, Maximillian, Alexander, and Benjamin.
Following their dreams, making the most of their individual odysseys.

VICTOR

Sleeping Bear Press wishes to thank and acknowledge Deirdre Menchaca
for reading and reviewing the manuscript.

Sleeping Bear Press™
310 North Main Street, Suite 300
Chelsea, MI 48118
www.sleepingbearpress.com

© 2008 Sleeping Bear Press is an imprint of Gale, a part of Cengage Learning.

Printed and bound in China.

10 9 8 7 6 5 4 3 2 1

Library of Congress Cataloging-in-Publication Data

Wilbur, Helen L., 1948-
Z is for Zeus : a Greek mythology alphabet / written by Helen L. Wilbur ;
illustrated by Victor Juhasz. — 1st ed.
p. cm.
Summary: "An A to Z introduction to Greek mythology including heroes, gods
and goddesses, the Iliad, Delphi, and Labyrinth. Each topic is introduced with a
poem and includes detailed-filled expository text"—Provided by publisher.
ISBN 978-1-58536-341-4
1. Mythology, Greek—Juvenile literature. I. Juhasz, Victor. II.
Title.
BL783.W55 2008
292.1'3—dc22   2007026155

Why It's Greek to You

Chances are you have encountered a Greek myth today. Many familiar words and names of organizations, companies, products, and places come from Greek myths. The planets and their moons are all named for gods and goddesses from Greek or Roman mythology. In fact, our word "alphabet" comes from *alpha* and *beta*, the first two letters of the Greek alphabet.

Many words we commonly use are derived from mythical names:

Akademos	A legendary hero	*academy, academic*
Hypnos	God of sleep	*hypnosis*
Narcissus	Youth obsessed with self-love	*narcissist*
Titans	Ancient race of giants	*titanic*
Zelos	God of great enthusiasm	*zeal*
Zephyrus	God of the West Wind	*zephyr*
Muses	Deities who inspired artists	*music, museum*
Phobos	God of fear	*phobia*
Pan	God of shepherds	*panic*

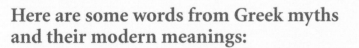

Here are some words from Greek myths and their modern meanings:

oracle: an authority or source of wise counsel and vision of the future

odyssey: a long, eventful trip

echo: a repeating sound

chaos: a state of disorder or confusion

labyrinth: a maze; a complex structure in which it is difficult to find your way

Names from mythology which you will recognize:

Amazon: Race of women warriors

Atlas: Titan who supported the earth on his shoulders

Nike: Goddess of Victory

Mentor: Friend and advisor to Odysseus

Nemesis: Goddess of Justice and Revenge

Ajax: Hero of great strength

Since before the time of Shakespeare, people have used the phrase "it's Greek to me" to mean something that is difficult or impossible to understand. Mythological terms are commonly used today. By reading and studying the myths and their culture you can expand your understanding of the words, their meanings, and symbols, making them no longer Greek to you.

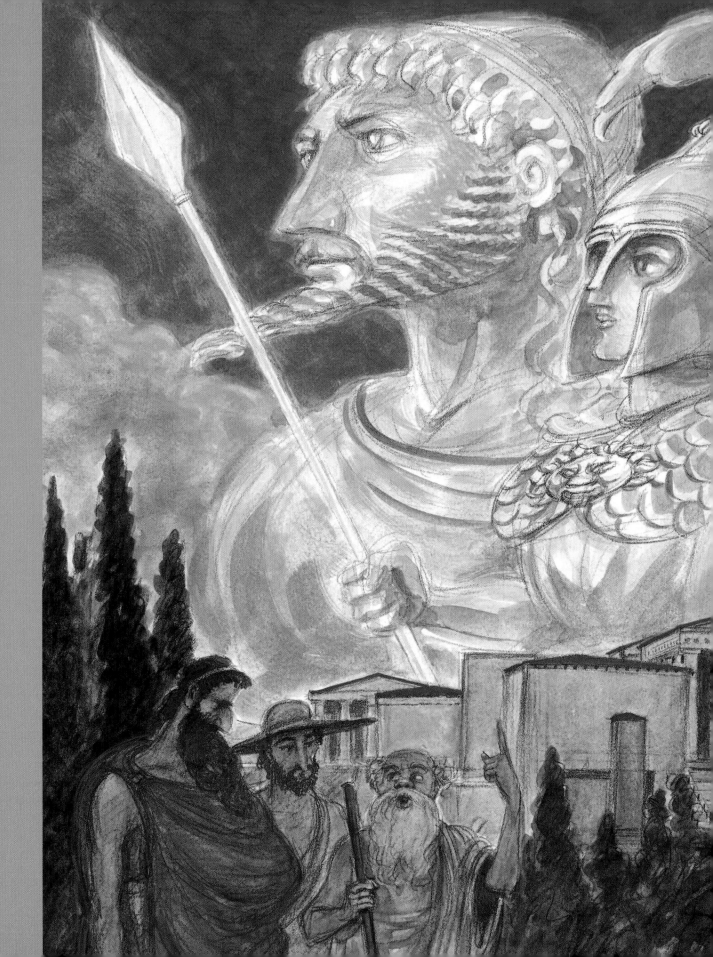

A a

Ancient Greece is often called "the cradle of Western civilization" because of its great influence on today's institutions and culture. The ideas, ideals, language, politics, poetry, theater, art, architecture, science, and philosophy of ancient Greece have helped to shape almost every aspect of modern life, from trial by jury to sporting competitions.

Ancient civilizations flourished over 4,000 years ago in the region we now know as modern Greece. Rugged mountains isolated the Greek Peninsula from the rest of Europe and the rough terrain made farming difficult. The long coastline with its many islands made the ancient Greeks excellent sailors and promoted fishing, trade, and colonization on the Aegean Sea.

Although the ancient Greeks shared a common culture, language, and religion, they were not living as citizens united into a single country. They lived in many independent city-states called *poli*, ruled by groups of aristocrats. The city-states developed alliances and rivalries and often very different characteristics.

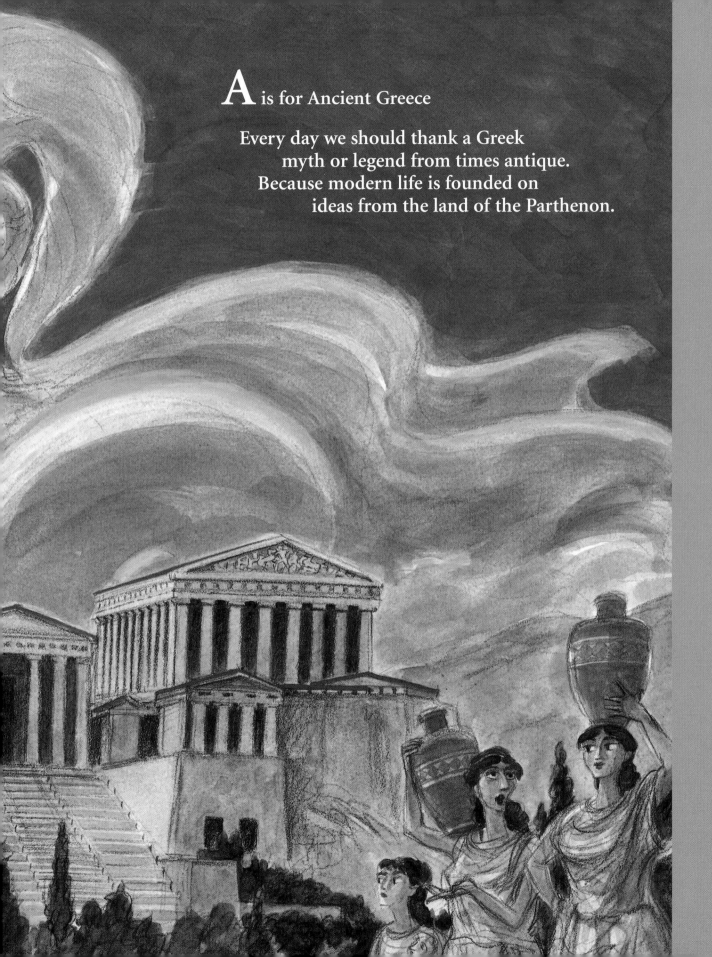

A is for Ancient Greece

Every day we should thank a Greek
myth or legend from times antique.
Because modern life is founded on
ideas from the land of the Parthenon.

By the sixth century BC two of the most powerful city-states were Athens and Sparta. Spartan life focused on discipline, hardship, and military service. At the age of seven, boys left their homes to be raised in barracks and train for the life of the soldier. Athens balanced commercial and military power with a life centered on the arts, philosophy, and learning. In 500 BC Athens established the world's first democracy. However, only free males participated in governing Athens—not women or slaves.

Greek life centered on the *agora*, or market, which served as a place for social meetings as well as the exchange of ideas. Many cities were built on high ground and enclosed with walls for defense. This type of fortified city was called an *acropolis*, meaning "high city." One of the most famous examples is the Acropolis in Athens. The Parthenon, a monumental temple to the city's patron goddess Athena, sits atop it and is recognized as a symbol of Greece around the world.

The ancient Greeks told stories, which we call myths, to explain the mysteries of the world around them. As part of this mythology they worshipped many gods. They attributed both beneficial and harmful natural events to the actions of their gods. These gods controlled everything—sunrise, sunset, rainbows, the seasons, winds, storms, and earthquakes—and also took part in the drama of human life.

B is for Beauties and Beasts

Gentle spirits wild and free,
daughters of the earth and sea.
By rushing stream and misty glen,
enchanting gods as well as men.

The world of ancient Greece was alive with supernatural beings and other fabulous creatures.

The god Apollo fell in love with the nymph Daphne but she fled from him. Just as Apollo caught her, Daphne cried to her father, the River God, for help and he turned her into a laurel tree. To honor Daphne, Apollo made the laurel his sacred tree and wore a crown of its leaves.

Nymphs were beautiful female spirits of nature who lived in trees, mountains, seas, and other wild places. These gentle deities often acted as companions to goddesses or nursemaids to divine offspring like Zeus and Dionysus. Their youth and beauty attracted the romantic attentions of gods as well as humans.

Centaurs and satyrs also lived in the woods and mountains. Centaurs (creatures with the head and torso of a man on the body of a horse) could be aggressive and violent, especially when drinking. An exception was the gentle centaur Chiron whose wisdom and knowledge of hunting and healing made him the tutor of many heroes like Jason and Achilles.

Satyrs had the legs, ears, and horns of a goat and the head and chest of a man. As companions of Dionysus, they spent their time dancing, drinking, and chasing nymphs. The satyr Pan, with his musical pipes, was god of the shepherds.

Bb

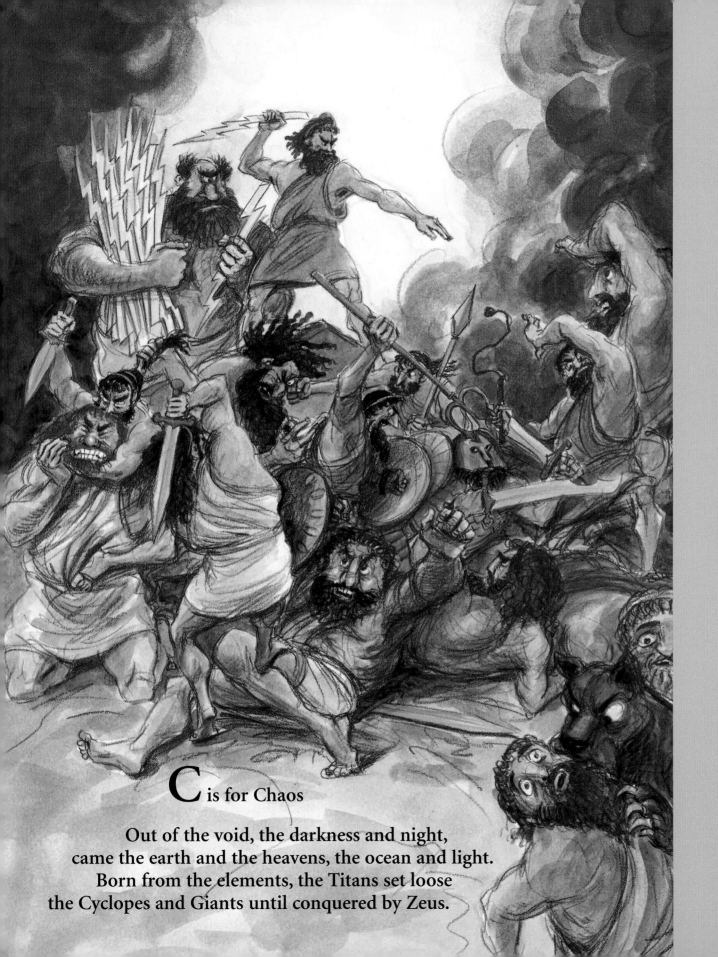

The ancient Greeks believed that, when the world began, everything emerged from Chaos, a vast and empty void. Chaos created Gaia, the earth, as well as Night, Darkness, Day, and Light. Gaia created the mountains, rivers, and sea, and, with the sky god, Uranus, gave birth to the Titans, Cyclopes, and Giants.

The gigantic, powerful race of Titans was the earliest generation of gods. They ruled the earth and married to produce the next generation of gods, the Olympians, as well as other gods and spirits, like the Furies. Cronus, the youngest son of Gaia and Uranus, overthrew his father to become the ruling Titan. In turn, Zeus, the youngest son of Cronus, rebelled against his father and the Titans. With the other Olympians, Zeus defeated the Titans in a huge battle aided by the thunderbolts made for him by the Cyclopes.

Zeus established himself as the ruler of the gods, banishing the Titans to Tartarus, the deepest part of the Underworld. As supreme god, he gave the realms of the ocean and underworld to his brothers Poseidon and Hades, and brought his favored siblings and children to live and rule with him on Mount Olympus.

C is for Chaos

Out of the void, the darkness and night,
came the earth and the heavens, the ocean and light.
Born from the elements, the Titans set loose
the Cyclopes and Giants until conquered by Zeus.

D is for Delphi

Oracle, tell me where should I roam?
Shall I travel to Thebes or stay close to home?
Will my destiny be humble or my glory be great?
Speak to me, Pythia, tell me my fate!

Zeus sent two swift eagles flying from the opposite ends of the universe to find the center of the earth and they met over Delphi. The ancient Greeks called it the *omphalos* or "navel of the world."

For the ancient Greeks, fate ruled the course of life for gods as well as humans. People consulted oracles and seers to understand the future course of events and get advice on how to avoid misfortune. No important job or undertaking was done before consulting an oracle.

Oracles were sacred shrines where the gods revealed fates to humans. At the Oracle of Delphi, the most well-known in ancient times, the priestess, called Pythia, sat on a tripod uttering predictions to those who consulted her. Her answers were often deceptive and puzzling, causing her human petitioners to misunderstand her instructions.

Oedipus consulted the Oracle and was told that he would kill his father and marry his mother. To avoid this terrible fate, he left his home in Corinth for the city of Thebes. What the Oracle failed to mention was that the king and queen of Corinth were not his real parents—the king and queen of Thebes were.

In Greek mythology Orpheus was the greatest poet and musician who ever lived. The Muses taught him to play the lyre so beautifully that he enchanted not only the birds and beasts but also the rocks and trees with his music. Orpheus loved his young wife, Eurydice, and was heartbroken when she stepped on a snake and died from its bite.

In his sorrow Orpheus traveled to the Underworld to plead with its king, Hades, to return Eurydice to life. Hades jealously guarded his kingdom and never allowed his subjects to leave. But Orpheus sang so mournfully of his lost love that all the spirits wept. Hades himself was moved and agreed to release her on one condition: "You may lead Eurydice out of my realm, but do not look back before she reaches the world of the living or she will be lost forever."

Eurydice followed Orpheus up the steep path and through the dark passages out of the Underworld. But just as Orpheus reached daylight, he forgot his pledge. He looked around to make sure his wife was behind him. Eurydice, who had not yet stepped into the sunshine, vanished into the Underworld forever.

E e

E is for Eurydice and Orpheus

You can take your wife from Hades's fold,
but don't forget that you've been told
"Don't look back"—for if you do,
Hades will take her back from you.

Ff

The Moirae, commonly known as the Fates, were three goddesses who determined the destiny of each individual at birth. Clotho, Lachesis, and Atropos spun, measured, and cut the thread of human life. Humans and gods would attempt to avoid or bargain with the Fates but their decisions were final. In the epic poem the *Iliad*, as the warrior Hector prepares for battle he soothes his worried wife by telling her if he is fated to die that day he will die whether he stays at home or goes to war. If he is not fated to die, then he will come to no harm in the battle.

Born from the blood of the Titan Uranus, the Erinyes, often called the Furies, were frightening spirits with snakes in their hair. They pursued and brought vengeance on those who committed crimes, especially against their own relatives.

Groups of goddesses with more appealing duties were the Muses and Graces. Daughters of Zeus, they dwelled on Mount Olympus with the other gods. The nine Muses presided over the arts and intellectual disciplines such as poetry and dance, as well as history, mathematics, and astronomy. Under the guidance of Apollo, they served as a source of inspiration for artists and scholars. The three Graces, associated with Aphrodite, represented feminine beauty, charm, and good cheer.

F is for the Fates

Though the Fates determine at your birth
your length of time upon this earth,
the Muses and Graces give you beauty and song
to bring you joy and make you strong.

G g

The gods and goddesses of ancient Greece appeared in human form but they remained forever young and beautiful. Although they, too, were subject to fate, they had more power and knowledge than human beings. Their ability to travel swiftly, invisibly, and change into different forms also gave them a big edge. They acted like people—they fell in love, married, had children, argued, cheated, lied, and took sides in human disputes.

Each deity had control over a different aspect of existence, and their activities shaped the rhythm of daily life. The Greeks thought the earth was flat, surrounded by the River Ocean. Every morning Eos, goddess of the dawn, rose to clear away the night, followed by her brother Helios, the sun god, who drove his golden chariot across the sky east to west. Their sister Selene, the moon goddess, made her journey across the night sky in a silver chariot after she bathed in the sea.

G is for Gods and Goddesses

To live forever looking good,
    reside in a heavenly neighborhood,
be superhuman, no stress or strife—
        To be a god, well…that's the life!

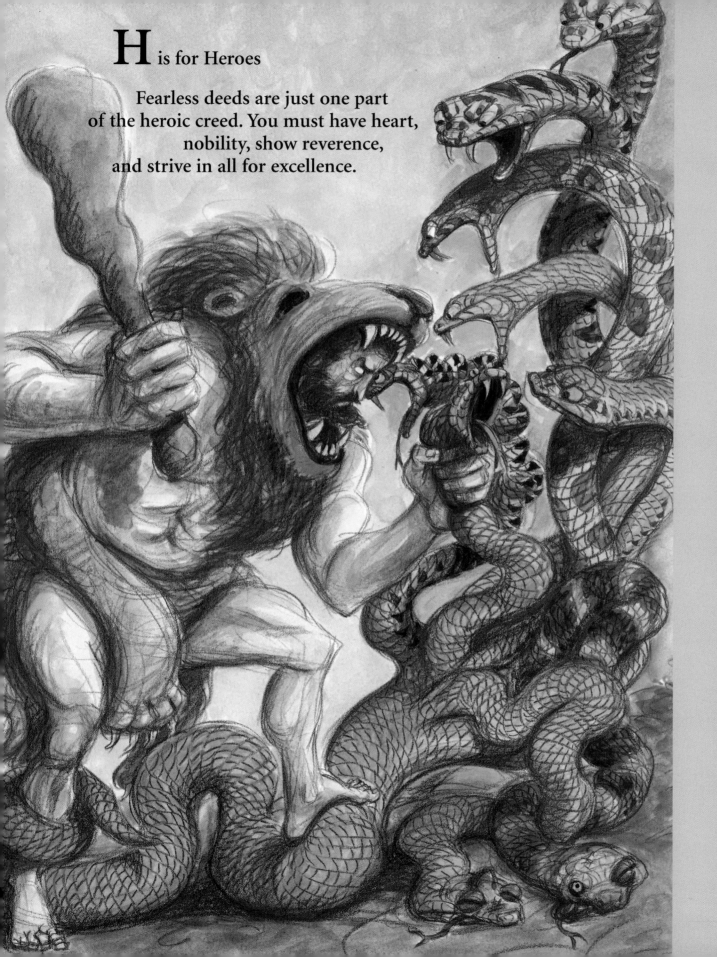

H is for Heroes

Fearless deeds are just one part
of the heroic creed. You must have heart,
nobility, show reverence,
and strive in all for excellence.

The Greek heroic ideal demanded physical and mental excellence (*areté*), nobility, honor, modesty, and humility (*aidos*). Brave deeds earned a hero glory and sometimes immortality. Many of the mythic heroes, Achilles, Perseus, Herakles, were the child of a god and a human. The gods often took sides to help or hinder heroes in their endeavors.

Many stories tell how Herakles ('Hercules' to the Romans) conquered numerous beasts, monsters, and human enemies. The famous Twelve Labors of Herakles were impossible tasks given to him to atone for mistakenly killing his family.

The Amazons, a race of fierce female warriors, fought in the Trojan War. Many myths show women of uncommon courage, intelligence, and devotion like Atalanta, Antigone, and Penelope. Antigone disobeyed a king's command to leave her brother unburied and was herself buried alive.

Why is a fatal flaw or weakness called an *Achilles' heel*? The great warrior Achilles was immune to harm because his mother, Thetis, dipped him in the enchanted waters of the River Styx, holding him by the heel. A poisoned arrow struck his unprotected heel and killed him.

The Greek gods and goddesses were all part of a huge extended family that began with Gaia and the Titans. Because many of them had children with mortals, as well as with each other, the family tree gets quite complicated and includes giants and monsters, as well as human heroes. Some of the families were also quite large—the Titans Oceanus and Tethys gave birth to all the 3,000 sea nymphs, called the Oceanids.

The gods were not models of good behavior. Their power was to be respected and feared. Religious practice focused on honoring and pleasing the gods in order to have a good life. Ancient Greeks built beautiful marble temples to worship their gods and made offerings, making a promise in return for a god's good favor.

People also held ceremonies, sacrifices, feasts, festivals, and athletic contests to honor their gods. Their most famous games, the Olympics honoring Zeus, began around 700 BC and continue today with many of the same sporting events: wrestling, running, jumping, and throwing the javelin and discus.

The epic poem, the *Iliad*, dates from the eighth century BC. The story takes place during the final year of the Trojan War when the Greeks, under King Agamemnon, attacked the city of Ilium, or Troy. Their goal was to retrieve Helen, who had been kidnapped from her home in Sparta. The Greek army is in trouble, however, because their great warrior, Achilles, feels that Agamemnon has insulted him and he refuses to fight.

Achilles and Agamemnon reconciled, but not before the Greeks suffered great losses in battle. Achilles returned to the battlefield and killed the great Trojan warrior Hector. Throughout the war, the gods took sides and helped their favorites until Zeus called a council on Olympus to stop their interfering.

When the blind poet Homer composed the *Iliad* 2,800 years ago, few people could read or write. Traveling poets performed their verses, often changing details according to the region or tastes of the audience. The beauty and clarity of the language, the vividness of the battles scenes and human drama, the depiction of the values and ideas of the time all contribute to making the *Iliad* one of the greatest and most enduring works of Western literature.

I is for the *Iliad*

The city has vanished, the battle is done.
The ships have departed, the warriors gone.
Only the words of a poet remain
to tell of the triumph, the sorrow, the pain.

Ii

J j

It is hard to believe that a beauty contest started a ten-year war. Eris, goddess of discord, upset that she had not been invited to a wedding on Olympus, tossed a golden apple labeled "For the Fairest" into the celebration. Squabbling broke out as goddesses competed for the apple. Zeus refused to judge the matter and gave the task to a handsome young shepherd named Paris.

Paris, the son of King Priam of Troy, had been hidden by shepherds to keep him from fulfilling the prophecy that he would bring about the downfall of Troy. Hera, Athena, and Aphrodite each tried to bribe him to win the prize.

Paris awarded the apple to Aphrodite since she had promised him Helen, the most beautiful woman in the world. Helen had an unusual background—she was born from an egg created when Zeus appeared to her mother, Leda, as a swan. Her stepfather, knowing beauty like Helen's could cause a lot of trouble, made her many suitors swear that they would stand by her chosen husband to protect her.

Helen married Menelaus, king of Sparta. When Paris visited Sparta and kidnapped Helen to Troy, the reluctant suitors had to fulfill their promise, thus starting the Trojan War.

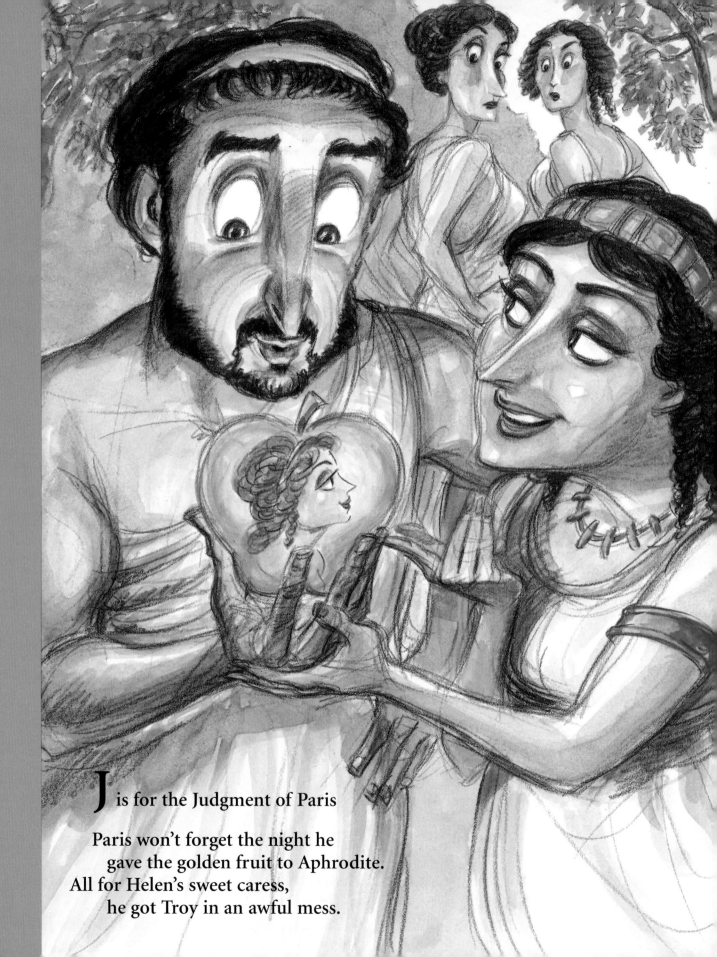

J is for the Judgment of Paris

Paris won't forget the night he
gave the golden fruit to Aphrodite.
All for Helen's sweet caress,
he got Troy in an awful mess.

King Midas was a man of pleasure who loved his celebrated rose garden. One day the satyr Silenus, tutor of Dionysus, wandered away from his rowdy companions and fell in a drunken stupor into Midas's roses. Silenus was brought before Midas, who took a liking to the old satyr and the stories he told. He entertained Silenus for several days, then returned him to Dionysus.

Dionysus had been worried about his old teacher. Relieved to have Silenus back safely, he asked Midas what reward he wanted. Midas replied "I want everything I touch to turn to gold!" Dionysus shook his head at the king's folly but granted the wish.

Midas couldn't believe it. He touched a stone, an apple, a tree—all turned to gold! Rejoicing, he entered his palace and turned all the furnishings into gold. He ordered a feast to celebrate his good fortune but found as he touched his food and wine, it turned to solid gold. He would starve!

In despair Midas appealed to Dionysus to reverse the gift. Laughing, Dionysus consented. "Go wash yourself in the River Pactolus and the gift will disappear."

So today when we say that someone has the "Midas touch," we mean that everything he or she does appears to be successful.

Kk

K is for King Midas

King Midas will tell you if you're very bold
and ask that all that you touch turns to gold,
what seems like a blessing will make you feel cursed.
You'll pray to the heavens to have it reversed.

The Minotaur was a fierce, bloodthirsty creature with the head of a bull and the body of a man. Minos, the king of Crete, imprisoned it in a labyrinth (maze) built by the inventor Daedalus. Anyone set into the labyrinth would get lost in its twisting corridors for the Minotaur to capture and eat alive.

Minos held Aegeus, the king of Athens, responsible for the death of his son, Androgeus. To make amends, every year Athens had to send seven youths and seven maidens to Crete to be fed to the Minotaur. Seeing the suffering of their families, Aegeus's son, Theseus, offered to go as one of the doomed youths, vowing to kill the Minotaur.

When Crete's royal court greeted the young Athenians destined for sacrifice, Minos's daughter, Ariadne, fell in love with Theseus. Ariadne knew the secrets of the labyrinth as Daedalus had told her how to navigate its passages with a magic ball of thread. Theseus promised to marry Ariadne and bring her back to Athens if she helped him kill the Minotaur.

Ariadne gave the thread and a sword to Theseus. Entering the labyrinth at night, he followed the magic ball of thread as it unwound through the maze and killed the sleeping Minotaur. Theseus fled to the harbor with Ariadne and the captives and set sail for Athens. Theseus was a hero, but not to Ariadne. On the way back to Athens, he broke his promise and left her as she slept on the island of Naxos.

Ll

L is for the Labyrinth

Inside the labyrinth's twisting maze,
  he hides apart from human gaze.
The most fearsome beast I ever saw:
  Half man, half bull–the Minotaur.

It's part of a hero's job to rid the world of monsters. Monsters can be giants with unusual features (100 hands, 50 heads) that make them difficult to destroy, or strange, dangerous beings with body parts from different animals like the Minotaur.

Echidna, the "Mother of all Monsters," was a combination of beautiful nymph and hideous serpent. Distant cousins to the other gods, Echidna and her mate, the huge and horrible Typhon, gave birth to a scary family, among them:

Cerberus: *This ferocious three-headed dog guarded the entrance to the Underworld.*

Chimera: *With three heads (a snake, a lion, and a goat), the chimera breathed fire until killed by Bellerophon.*

Lernean Hydra: *Its serpent body topped by nine poisonous heads, the hydra had breath so foul it killed men and beasts.*

Nemean Lion: *Herakles strangled this enormous lion whose hide was impervious to any weapon.*

Sphinx: *Oedipus finally vanquished this infamous riddler.*

Zeus overcame Typhon in a monumental battle. He let Echidna and her offspring live to challenge future heroes.

M
m

M is for Monster

With serpent's teeth and fiery breath
hissing and spitting destruction and death,
it slithers from its dark domain.
Slay the monster or be slain!

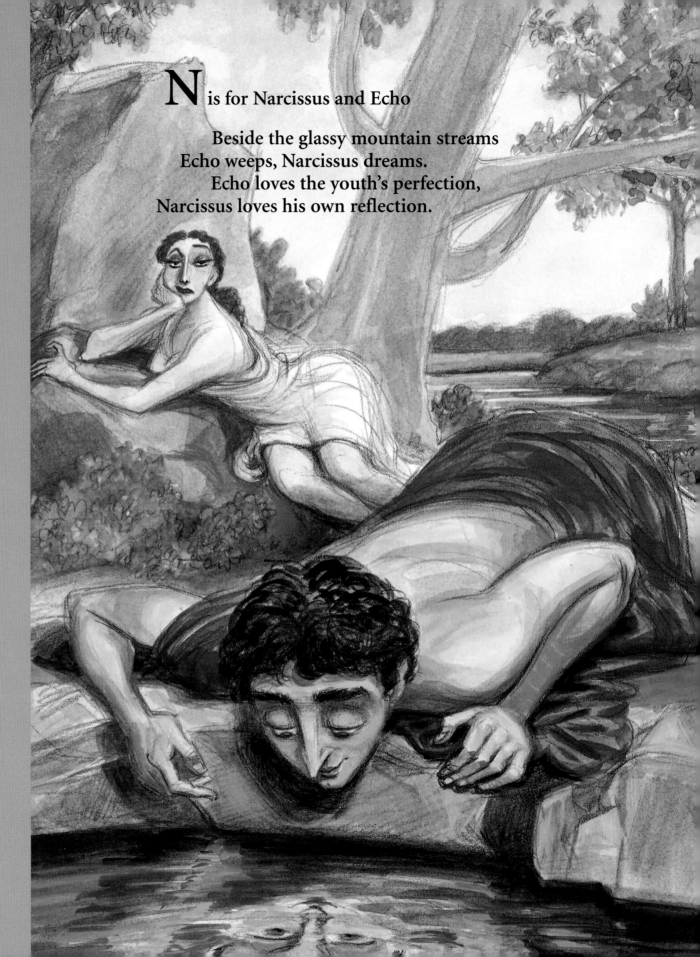

N is for Narcissus and Echo

Beside the glassy mountain streams
Echo weeps, Narcissus dreams.
Echo loves the youth's perfection,
Narcissus loves his own reflection.

Echo was a beautiful nymph whose constant chatter got her into trouble. She talked so much that she distracted Hera from discovering that Zeus was having secret love affairs. Hera was furious when she found out and punished Echo by taking away her ability to speak first. She could only repeat the words said to her.

Echo fell in love with a vain, handsome youth named Narcissus. Anyone who saw him immediately fell in love with him, but Narcissus loved no one. Echo pursued him but Narcissus rejected her and she could only repeat the cruel words he said to her. Echo faded away from longing and loneliness until only her voice remained.

Narcissus broke one heart too many and one of his rejected suitors asked the gods to punish him. Walking in the woods one day, Narcissus looked into a clear pool and fell in love with his own reflection. Eventually, he gazed so long at his image in the pool that he, too, faded away. When the nymphs went to find him, all they found was a beautiful white flower we call a narcissus.

In Greek mythology the Olympians were the 12 supreme gods and goddesses who ruled the universe from the top of Mount Olympus, after the fall of the Titans. At different times, different gods were recognized under this title; however, the 12 names listed below are the ones most often considered Olympians.

Along with **Zeus** (he gets his own letter in **Z**), Hera, Poseidon, and Demeter were siblings and the children of the Titans Cronus and Rhea.

Hera, wife of Zeus and queen of Olympus, was the goddess of marriage and childbirth. Zeus's romantic adventures kept Hera busy tracking down and punishing her rivals and their children.

Poseidon, god of the seas, earthquakes, and horses, lived in a palace of coral and gold on the ocean floor. He gave safe passage to ships and rode in a chariot pulled by horses or a hippocampus (half horse, half sea serpent).

Demeter, goddess of grain and fertility, ruled over the fruits of the earth and the harvest.

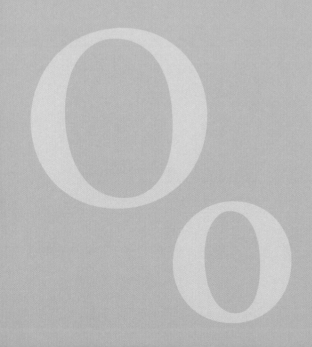

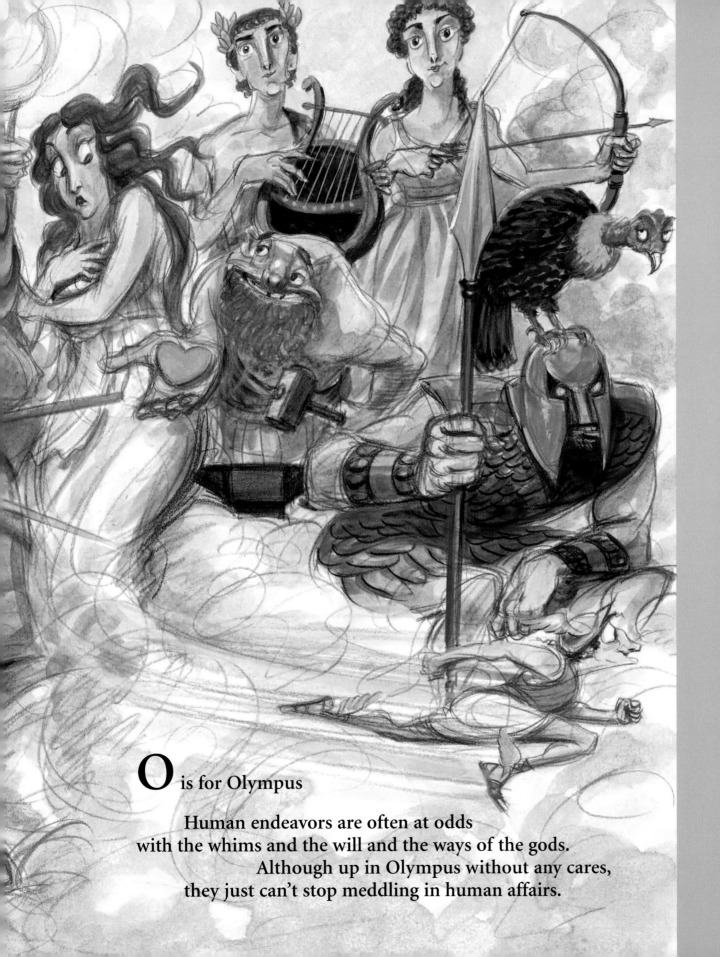

Aphrodite, goddess of love and beauty, was born from the foam of the sea.

The goddess **Athena** sprang fully grown, and fully armed, from the head of her father, Zeus. Favorite child of Zeus, Athena represented wisdom and civilized life.

Zeus fathered the twins **Apollo** and **Artemis**. One of the most important and widely worshipped gods, Apollo was the god of archery, prophecy, medicine, and music. Artemis, goddess of the hunt and the wild, traveled in the woods with her nymphs.

Hermes, messenger of the gods, used his winged sandals to give him great speed. He was the god of merchants and thieves and escorted dead souls to the Underworld.

Ares, god of war, and **Hephaestus**, god of fire and craftsmen, were sons of Zeus and Hera. At his forge Hephaestus produced important equipment for the other gods such as their weapons, armor, arrows, and chariots, as well as the shield and thunderbolts of Zeus.

Dionysus, god of wine, had many followers and festivals. As the "party god," Dionysus was also patron deity of the theater.

With Zeus as their king, these immortals lived in splendid palaces high in the clouds. The food and drink of the gods on Olympus, nectar and ambrosia, maintained their immortality. Family life on Olympus was complex and often quarrelsome.

O is for Olympus

Human endeavors are often at odds
with the whims and the will and the ways of the gods.
Although up in Olympus without any cares,
they just can't stop meddling in human affairs.

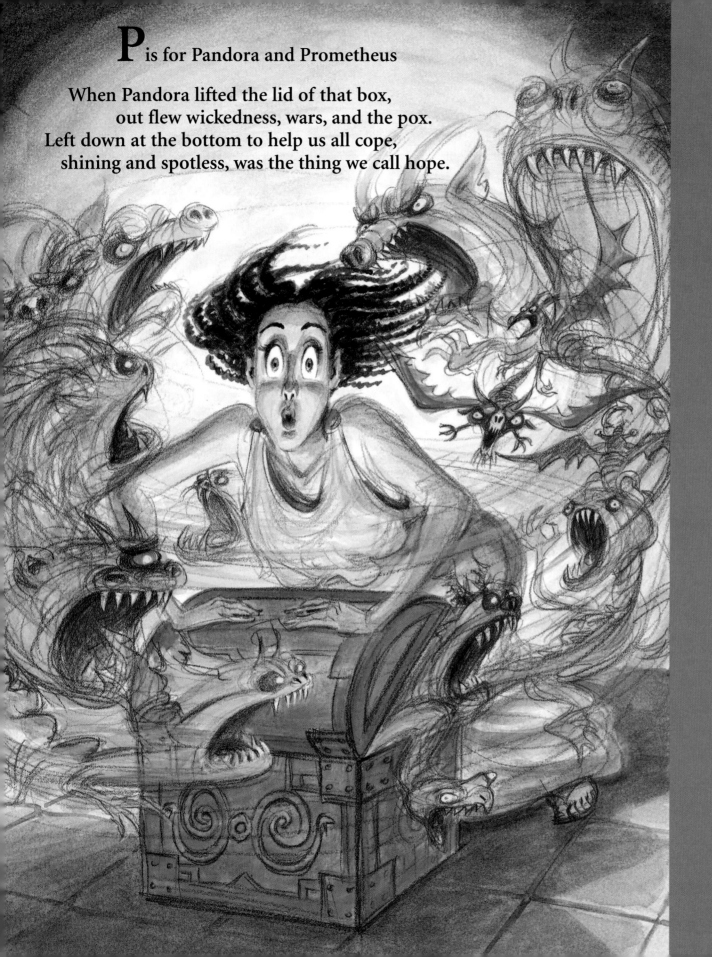

P is for Pandora and Prometheus

When Pandora lifted the lid of that box,
out flew wickedness, wars, and the pox.
Left down at the bottom to help us all cope,
shining and spotless, was the thing we call hope.

Pp

Prometheus, one of the Titans, helped Zeus triumph over Cronus; however, he later rebelled by stealing fire from the gods and giving it to mankind as a gift. As punishment, Prometheus was chained to a rock where an eagle pecked at him. Since he was immortal, his torment was never-ending.

Zeus then had Hephaestus create a woman, Pandora, to whom the gods gave gifts of beauty, grace, charm, and persuasion. Zeus endowed her with curiosity. Prometheus had warned his brother, Epithemeus, never to accept a gift from Zeus. But when Zeus offered Pandora to Epithemeus, he fell in love and married her.

Along with Pandora, Zeus sent a box which he said must never be opened. But Pandora's curiosity got the better of her. She opened the box and the evils of the world—sickness, war, insanity, and strife—all flew out. Pandora quickly shut the lid but all the misery and hardship had escaped. Only one thing remained at the bottom of the box—hope.

What happened to Prometheus? Eventually Zeus took pity on him and had Herakles kill the eagle, releasing Prometheus from his suffering.

Heroes often get sent on impossible quests to kill a ferocious monster or obtain a priceless treasure (guarded by a ferocious monster). Often the person initiating the quest assumes that the hero will perish in the process.

King Pelias seized his brother's kingdom. One day his nephew Jason showed up to reclaim the throne. Pelias told Jason he would step down if Jason could retrieve the Golden Fleece. It hung from a tree in the land of Colchis, guarded by a dragon that never slept.

After consulting the Oracle, Jason assembled an all-star team of 50 heroes called the Argonauts, after their ship, the *Argos*. The team included Castor, Pollux, Orpheus, Herakles, Peleus (the father of Achilles), and one woman, Atalanta.

In Colchis the king had a daughter, Medea, who was a sorceress. She fell in love with Jason, used her sorcery to help him win the Golden Fleece, and returned with him to his kingdom. Jason married Medea but discovered that life with a witch has its difficulties. Medea, jealous and vengeful, gruesomely killed those who got in her way, including her own children by Jason.

Q is for Quest

Our quest is for the fleece of gold.
Our ship is swift…our spirits bold!
As Argonauts we will fulfill
this test of courage, strength, and will!

R r

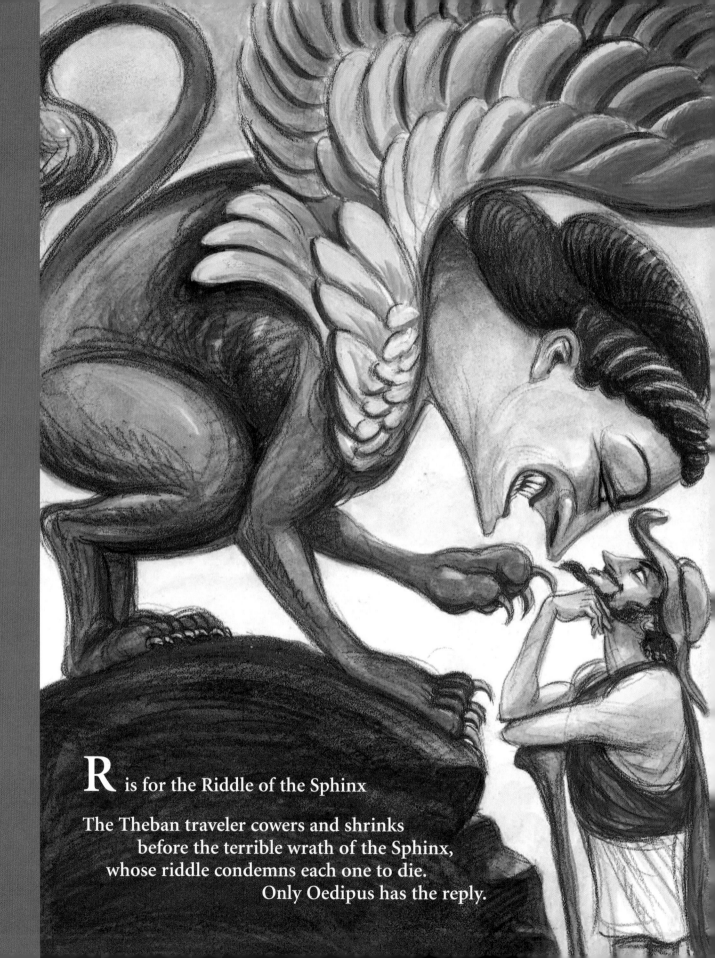

The city of Thebes had a problem. Hera sent the monstrous Sphinx to punish the city. Made up of a woman's head, a lion's body, and an eagle's wings, the Sphinx crouched on a rock on the road leading into Thebes. She stopped all travelers and asked them to solve a riddle, killing those who failed to answer correctly. No one had solved the riddle; no one could attempt to enter the city without being killed.

Oedipus, trying to escape a dire fate predicted by the Oracle, arrived on the road on his way to Thebes. The Sphinx leapt in front of him.

"What goes on four legs in the morning, two legs at noon, and three legs in the evening?"

Oedipus feared no man or monster and answered: "Man—who crawls on his hands and knees as a baby, walks on two feet as an adult, and leans on a cane in old age."

Mortified that the riddle was solved, the Sphinx flung herself into the valley and perished. The grateful people of Thebes proclaimed Oedipus their king, bringing him closer to his unfortunate fate.

R is for the Riddle of the Sphinx

The Theban traveler cowers and shrinks
before the terrible wrath of the Sphinx,
whose riddle condemns each one to die.
Only Oedipus has the reply.

Look up into the night sky and you can see the myths come to life. One of the easiest constellations to recognize by the three bright stars that make up his belt is the hunter Orion. Artemis fell in love with the handsome hunter but mistakenly killed him with an arrow on a dare from her brother, Apollo. Moved by her grief, Zeus placed Orion in the sky.

Close to Orion is his dog *Canis Major* which features Sirius, the brightest star in the sky. Other constellations are named for gods or creatures the gods made immortal by placing them in the heavens.

The ancient Greeks watched the heavens closely, recognizing that the positions of the stars and other heavenly bodies indicated the change of the seasons and weather. Planets, from the Greek *planetos* meaning "wanderers," appeared to wander among the stars. These observations helped them know when to plant and harvest crops, move flocks, and how to navigate the seas.

Ancient people grouped stars into picture patterns called constellations to help them remember how and where the stars were located and to follow their movements. Modern astronomy has a set of 88 constellations, many of which are those identified by the ancient Greeks.

S s

S is for Sirius, the brightest star in the sky

Above us in the starry night
the scorpion stings, the swan takes flight,
Orion hunts, the bear runs far,
spinning round the polar star.

T is for the Trojan Horse

The men of Troy took up their spears
    and fought the Greeks for ten long years.
One thing that they learned, of course—
    Do not bring home a wooden horse!

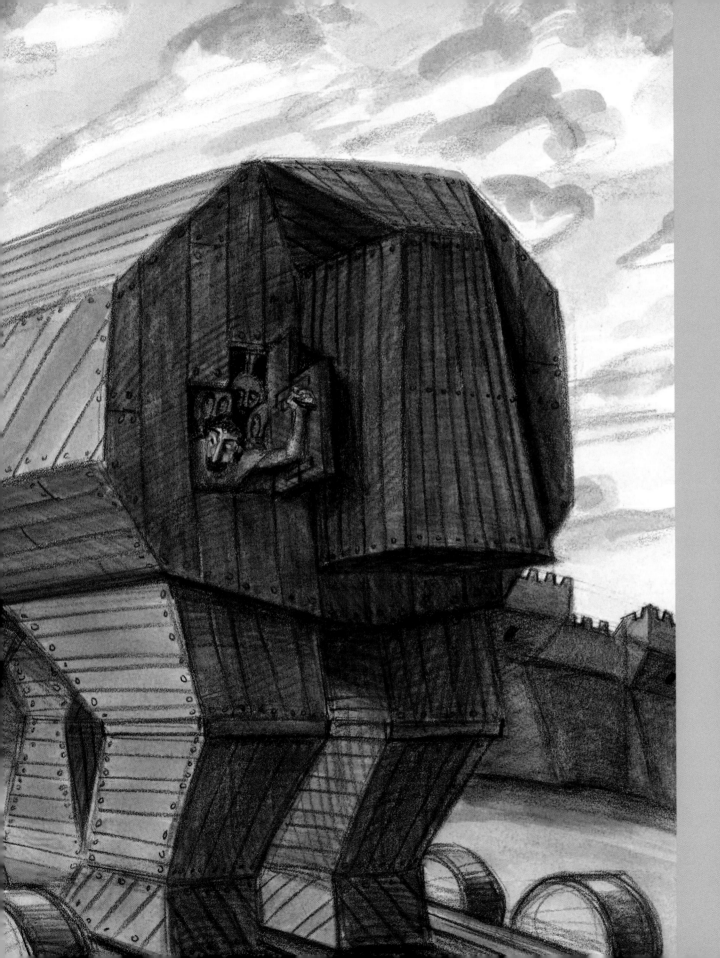

Tt

The Greeks laid siege to the city of Troy for ten years with much loss of life but victory for neither side.

In order to capture Troy by surprise, the Greeks built a huge wooden horse. It was constructed hollow so that soldiers could hide in it. The Greeks pretended to sail away from Troy, leaving the horse behind as a gift and offering to the gods.

The Trojans, celebrating the end of the long war, dragged the horse into the city walls and left it while they had a huge banquet. Night fell and while the people of Troy slept, the Greeks crept out of the horse. They killed the guards at the gate and let in the other warriors who had sailed back during the night.

Troy fell, Helen was returned to her husband, Menelaus, and the Greeks returned home in triumph.

A "Trojan horse" is something which appears innocent but contains dangerous or malicious effects. And the saying "Beware of Greeks bearing gifts" advises us to be mistrustful of gifts from our enemies.

Hades, the brother of Zeus, ruled the realm of the dead known as the Underworld. Like its king, this was a forbidding, dark, and gloomy place.

Spirits of the dead entered the Underworld by paying the ferryman, Charon, to take them across the river Acheron in his boat. Relatives placed a coin in the mouth of the deceased to pay their passage. Cerberus, a ferocious three-headed dog, guarded the gates to the Underworld to make sure no one left.

Hades wanted Persephone, the daughter of Demeter, to be his bride; however, her mother would never consent to have her beautiful child live in such a dismal place. When Hades kidnapped Persephone, Demeter, goddess of the harvest, searched everywhere for her lost child. In her grief, Demeter neglected the earth, bringing drought and famine.

Zeus finally put an end to this situation by sending Hermes to retrieve Persephone.

U u

U is for the Underworld

Welcome gentlemen, welcome ladies,
        to the Underworld, to the realm of Hades.
        It's cold and dark but do not grieve.
        Just don't get up and try to leave.

While in the Underworld, Persephone had eaten food (a few pomegranate seeds) which meant she could never fully leave. Hades compromised and kept his Queen Persephone with him part of the year (fall and winter). When Persephone returned to her mother each spring and summer the earth rejoiced, producing flowers and crops.

For most of the dead the Underworld was not a place of punishment or reward. Only the most wicked were singled out to go to the lowest depths of Tartarus where the Olympians had locked away the Titans. For stealing their nectar and ambrosia, the gods condemned Tantalus to be submerged to his neck unable to drink the water or to reach the juicy grapes over his head—forever "tantalized" but always thirsty and hungry.

The gods granted immortality to the greatest heroes, like Achilles, sending them to live forever in bliss in the Elysian Fields.

From ancient times the Greeks have a great tradition as a seafaring nation. With the longest coastline in Europe, they became expert mariners for trading, fishing, defense, and discovery. It's no wonder that many of their myths and legends feature great sea voyages.

Odysseus, clever as well as courageous, designed the Trojan horse which allowed the Greek army to conquer Troy. Sailing for home after the war, Odysseus and his crew encountered many dangers and adventures: man-eating monsters, shipwrecks, beautiful sorceresses, storms, and angry gods.

The Sirens (part woman, part bird) led sailors to shipwreck and death with their alluring songs. To pass their perilous island, Odysseus sealed his crew's ears with wax. He had the crew bind him to the mast so he could hear the Sirens' song without being lured into the sea.

Homer's epic, the *Odyssey*, tells the story of Odysseus's voyage home to his kingdom and wife Penelope after the Trojan War. In many languages, the word *odyssey* has come to mean a long and eventful journey, and is one of the most popular boat names.

V is for Voyage

Escaping Circe and the Sirens' song,
the one-eyed giant, the cannibal throng,
Odysseus sailed the restless sea,
home to Ithaca and Penelope.

W is for Water

Lord Poseidon, accept our praise.
Bring starlit nights and breezy days.
Calm the tempest, hear our plea.
Protect our ship from your storm-tossed sea.

Second in power only to his brother Zeus, Poseidon ruled the waters, earthquakes, and horses. He lived in a castle of coral in the depths of the sea. Poseidon calmed the sea when he rode the waves in a gold chariot pulled by white horses with bronze hooves and golden manes. He helped sailors to travel safely and fishermen to fill their nets.

Poseidon was known to have an unruly nature and violent temper. He directed his fury at mortals or gods who did not show him proper respect. He used his mighty trident, a three-pronged spear, to shake the waters and earth, creating floods and shipwrecks.

Poseidon created all the sea creatures and sent the dolphin, Delphinius, to help him court the nymph, Amphitrite, to be his wife. Like Zeus, Poseidon fathered many children by different goddesses and women. His offspring included the hunter Orion, as well as creatures like the winged horse, Pegasus; Triton, half man and half fish; and the sea monster, Charybdis.

W
W

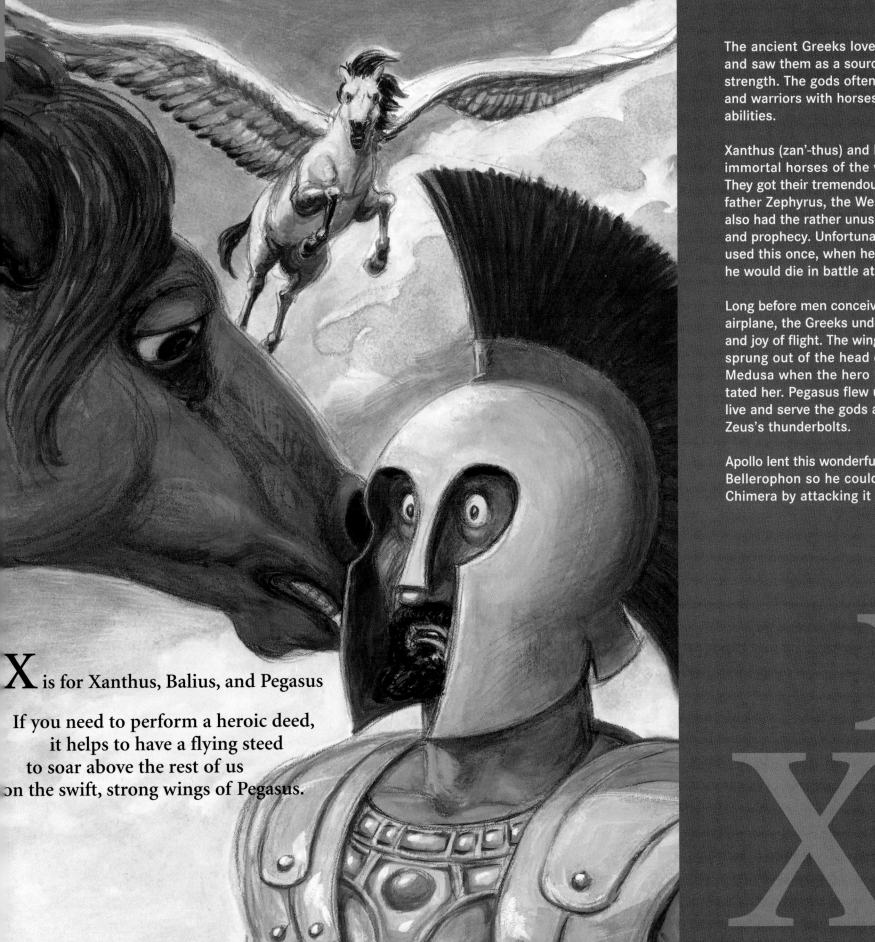

The ancient Greeks loved their horses and saw them as a source of courage and strength. The gods often supplied heroes and warriors with horses having fabulous abilities.

Xanthus (zan'-thus) and Balius were the immortal horses of the warrior Achilles. They got their tremendous speed from their father Zephyrus, the West Wind. Xanthus also had the rather unusual gifts of speech and prophecy. Unfortunately, Xanthus only used this once, when he warned Achilles he would die in battle at Troy.

Long before men conceived of flying in an airplane, the Greeks understood the power and joy of flight. The winged horse Pegasus sprung out of the head of the gorgon Medusa when the hero Perseus decapitated her. Pegasus flew up to Olympus to live and serve the gods as the carrier of Zeus's thunderbolts.

Apollo lent this wonderful horse to the hero Bellerophon so he could kill the monster Chimera by attacking it from above.

X is for Xanthus, Balius, and Pegasus

If you need to perform a heroic deed,
it helps to have a flying steed
to soar above the rest of us
on the swift, strong wings of Pegasus.

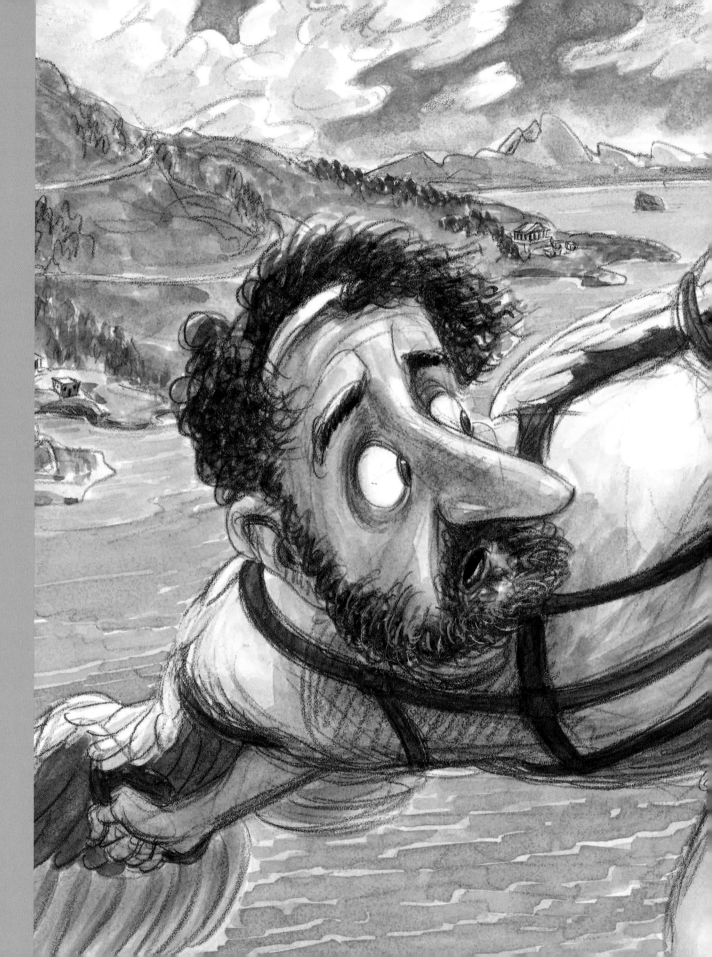

Yy

The ancient Greeks worshipped youth. Hebe, the goddess of youth, was cupbearer to the gods and brought them ambrosia. The gods granted their favorites eternal youth as well as eternal life. (What fun is it to live forever if you are going to be old for most of it?) But youth, although beautiful and strong, can be hasty and reckless.

Daedalus needed to flee the island of Crete with his son, Icarus. King Minos had figured out that he had given the secret of the labyrinth to Ariadne and Theseus, allowing them to kill the Minotaur and escape. Minos had the harbors and boats under guard so Daedalus built feather wings, held together with wax, to escape by air. Tying the wings to his and Icarus's arms, he warned: "If you fly too close to the water, the feathers will get wet. If you fly too close to the sun, the wax will melt. Follow me safely at a reasonable height."

Seeing them soar upward, the farmers in their fields and the fishermen on the sea mistook them for gods. Excited by the freedom of flight, Icarus disobeyed his father and flew higher and higher. As the sun warmed the wings, the wax melted. Icarus plummeted into the sea.

When Daedalus looked back, all he saw were white feathers floating on the blue water.

Y is for Youth

So calm the sea, so clear the sky,
a perfect day to learn to fly!
But please, my child, my precious one,
do not fly too close to the sun.

After his triumph over the Titans, Zeus made himself the supreme god and ruler of Olympus. As god of the sky, he controlled the weather—thunder, lightning, and rain. Although ruler of the gods and men, Zeus had little control over fate and destiny.

Zeus maintained justice by rewarding good rulers and punishing bad ones. He was especially severe on liars and humans arrogant enough to behave like gods (a characteristic called hubris). Zeus gave special protection to travelers and guests, often traveling in disguise to reward people who treated strangers with hospitality and kindness.

Zeus's family life was not always harmonious. He had many children, both human and divine, by goddesses as well as mortal women. Among others, he fathered Apollo, Artemis, Hebe, Persephone, Dionysus, the Fates, the Graces, the Muses, Herakles, and Helen of Troy. This was a source of constant conflict with his wife, Hera, who jealously pursued and punished his favorites and their children. In order to escape detection, Zeus frequently changed his form, appearing at times as a bull, an eagle, and even a shower of gold.

Zeus's symbols were the golden eagle, the oak tree, and the thunderbolt which he used to maintain supremacy and destroy his enemies. He also had a magical shield called the *aegis*, fashioned by Hephaestus and decorated with the head of Medusa.

Z is for Zeus

I rule the earth, I rule the sky.
I watch all with an eagle eye.
I'm the one who sets the thunderbolts loose.
I'm the king of the gods. Just call me Zeus!

Zz

Glossary of the Gods

The ancient Greeks depicted their gods and goddesses in sculpture and paintings on pottery. The architecture of their temples and public buildings inspired centuries of buildings. These beautiful objects still delight us today and have had a profound influence on Western art.

Since the Greeks pictured their gods as perfect beings, the figures don't look like real people and are difficult to tell apart. Their symbols can help you recognize the various gods and goddesses in paintings and sculpture. (The Romans adopted many of the Greek gods and goddesses but gave them different names.)

This chart will help you figure out who's who:

God or Goddess	Description	Symbols
Zeus (zoos)	God of the sky, ruler of Olympus	Thunderbolt, eagle, oak tree
Hera (hir'-uh)	Goddess of marriage	Crown, peacock, cow
Artemis (ahr'-tuh-mis)	Goddess of the hunt	Deer, cypress tree, bow
Demeter (dih-mee'-tur)	Goddess of agriculture	Torch, sheaf of wheat
Athena (a-thee'na)	Goddess of wisdom and culture	Owl, shield, olive tree
Hermes (hur'-meez)	Messenger of the gods	Winged sandals and helmet
Dionysus (dy-uh-ny'-suhs)	God of wine	Grapevine, ivy, wand
Apollo (a-pol'-lo)	God of light, prophecy, and healing	Bow, lyre, laurel, dolphin
Poseidon (puh-sy'-duhn)	Ruler of the sea	Trident, horse
Aphrodite (af-roh-dy'-tee)	Goddess of love and beauty	Dove, myrtle, swan
Ares (air'-eez)	God of war	Spear, vulture, dog
Hephaestus (huh-fes'-tuhs)	God of fire and forge	Anvil, forge